ITEM   021 346 520

cool science

D1428708

lcox

UXBRIDGE COLLEGE
LEARNING CENTRE

LERNER BOOKS • LONDON • NEW YORK • MINNEAPOLIS

First published in the United Kingdom in 2008 by
Lerner Books,
Dalton House,
60 Windsor Avenue,
London SW19 2RR

Website address: www.lernerbooks.co.uk

This edition was updated and edited for UK publication by Discovery Books Ltd.,
Unit 3, 37 Watling Street, Leintwardine, Shropshire SY7 0LW

British Library Cataloguing in Publication Data

Wilcox, Charlotte
Recycling. - (Cool science)
1. Recycling (Waste, etc.) - Juvenile literature
I. Title
628.4'458

ISBN-13: 978 1 58013 427 9

Printed in China

Table of Contents

Introduction · 4

chapter 1 · 8
Rubbish Rags

chapter 2 · 16
Making the Most of Muck

chapter 3 · 24
E-waste and E-cycling

chapter 4 · 30
New Uses for Old Tyres

chapter 5 · 37
Turning Rubbish
into Crude Oil

Glossary · 42
Selected Bibliography · · · · · · · · · · 44
Further Reading and Websites · · · · 46
Index · 47

Introduction

Every year people living in the UK use more than 13 billion plastic carrier bags, 12.5 billion tonnes of paper and 275 thousand tonnes of plastic bottles. We use most of this stuff once, then throw it away. Cars, mobile phones and computers last longer – maybe a few years. Still, every year thousands of these items are also thrown away.

Where do we put all this unwanted stuff? It's a huge problem. Leaving rubbish out in the open is illegal. It encourages pests and spreads diseases. Most rubbish goes to landfills, where it is buried underground. The bottom of a landfill is lined with waterproof

IT'S A FACT!

The United Kingdom produces around 430 million tonnes of waste every year. Around 30 million tonnes of this is produced in our homes. However, we are beginning to recycle more. Across the UK we are recycling around 25 per cent of our rubbish.

material to stop dangerous liquids leaking into the environment.

New rubbish arrives every day and workers add more soil to cover it. As the rubbish keeps coming, workers must pile landfills higher or spread them out over more land. Over time they get too big to manage and have to close.

When landfills close, cities and towns need new ones. They must be nearby so lorries don't have to travel too far with the rubbish.

It is also very expensive to put rubbish in landfills. Burying tonnes

IT'S A FACT!

We use more than 250 million plastic carrier bags a week in the UK. Each one will take hundreds of years to rot away in a landfill site.

You can reuse your plastic bags by taking them with you the next time you go shopping. Or, use your own bags or holdalls. Many supermarkets now offer customers bags for life. These harder–wearing plastic bags are reusable.

This landfill worker is burying rubbish underground to cover the smell and keep animals away.

of rubbish every day takes lots of workers, machines and fuel. Landfills take up valuable land that people could use for homes, farms and businesses, or that could simply be left unspoilt. Throwing away less rubbish means we need fewer landfills.

Recycling is one way to keep rubbish out of landfills. Paper, plastic, aluminium cans and steel car frames are some of the most frequently

Fresh Kills Landfill

New York City's largest landfill covers about 890 hectares. It is one of only a few artificial structures visible from outer space. Fresh Kills Landfill closed in March 2001 after more than fifty years of piling up rubbish. After the September 11, 2001, attacks on the World Trade Center in New York, Fresh Kills reopened to take the rubbish from the collapsed Twin Towers. Much of the rubbish was later recycled.

Fresh Kills Landfill is closed again now, for good. The city plans to turn it into a park. It will include two artificial hills. They'll be the size and shape of the World Trade Center towers laid on their sides. People will be able to climb to the tops of the hills. From there they'll be able to see the part of New York City where the towers once stood.

At Fresh Kills Landfill, piles of debris from New York City's Twin Towers frame a view of the city's skyline.

The Recycling Circle

Collecting

People collect recyclable items at homes, schools and businesses. They take the items to collection centres or refuse collectors pick up the items.

Processing

Recyclable rubbish goes to a recycling centre for sorting and processing. Workers and machines shred, chop or wash some materials. Machines press each type of material into bales or tightly-bound bundles.

Selling

Recycling centres sell bales to manufacturers (businesses that make things).

Manufacturing

Manufacturers use the materials to make new products. These include packaging, cloth, paper products and building materials.

Reusing

People buy products made from recycled materials, completing the circle. Some materials, like paper and aluminium, can go around the circle several times.

recycled items. They're mostly recycled into more of the same things. For example, used paper becomes new paper. Old aluminium cans make new aluminium cans.

People are coming up with creative new ways to recycle. These ideas turn old rubbish into completely different new things. For example, plastic bottles can become T-shirts. Tyres can turn into floors. Rotten waste can make energy to power homes and businesses.

Recycling can turn rubbish into valuable resources that we can use. That's what this book is about.

chapter 1

Rubbish Rags

Recycling old clothing isn't a new idea. People have been cutting up worn-out clothes to make quilts, rugs and cleaning rags for a long time. Making new clothes out of other kinds of rubbish is a very new idea. It helps the environment by using things that would otherwise go in landfills. Companies make clothing, hats, shoes and luggage from all sorts of rubbish.

Turning Bottles into Clothes

The kind of rubbish that most often becomes clothing is polyethylene terephthalate (PET-1 or PETE). People make clear drinks bottles from this particular type of plastic. A special type of PET-1 is used to make the sails on sailing boats. We can recycle PET-1 into not only cloth, but carpet as well. It is also often used to make the inside stuffing for jackets, sleeping bags or quilts and pillows.

This plant sorts different plastic products so they can be recycled and used again.

PET-1 plastic usually arrives at the recycling centre mixed with other plastic things (HDPE is another recyclable plastic). All the plastics need sorting. The different colours of PET-1 must be separated. In many recycling centres, workers sort the plastics by hand. Some centres use X-ray or infrared sensors (tools that see differences in light that our eyes can't see) to help with sorting. Computers read information from the sensors to find even tiny bits of non-PET-1 material.

Next the PET-1 containers go into a machine that crushes them together into bales. The bales go to another place for more sorting. They still have some non-PET-1 materials in them. These include missed bottle tops, labels and glue, as well as small amounts of drinks or food. Workers and machines sort, wash and dry the flattened containers.

Machines will shred the plastic in this bale (*left*) into flakes (*right*).

When the sorting and cleaning are done, machines shred the containers to make PET-1 flakes or pellets. Manufacturers continue the recycling process by buying pure PET-1 flakes. Most PET-1 flakes go to cloth makers.

The most common fabric made from recycled PET-1 is polyester. To make polyester thread, machines force melted PET-1 through a spinneret. The spinneret is a tool with many tiny holes in it, like a showerhead. As the liquid plastic sprays through the holes, it forms strands. The strands dry and twist together into polyester thread.

Bigger holes make thicker strands, and smaller holes make thinner strands. Thicker strands make thicker thread. The thicker the thread, the heavier the cloth it makes.

Polyester thread from clear PET-1 can be bleached white or dyed any colour. Thread from coloured PET-1 won't bleach, so it can only be dyed dark colours. After the thread is bleached or dyed, it's ready for knitting or weaving into cloth. The cloth can become shirts, sweatshirts, underwear, safety vests, jackets, hats or gloves.

A lot of polyester comes from recycled plastic. It's no surprise. Polyester from recycled PET-1 is exactly like polyester made from raw PET-1. If the shirt you're wearing contains polyester, it may be made from recycled bottles and jars. You're keeping plastic out of landfills by wearing it.

A worker watches a machine weave recycled PET-1 thread into polyester fabric at this plant in Indonesia.

Another kind of cloth made from recycled plastic is non-woven fabric. Woven fabric is made by knitting or weaving threads together. To make non-woven fabric, machines spread out thin sheets (called webs) of melted, tangled plastic strands. After the webs are cool and dry, machines roll them into sheets.

Non-woven fabric is made like paper and looks like paper, but it's much stronger. Non-woven fabric is almost impossible to tear, but is easy to cut with scissors. Clothes made from it are light and comfortable. Non-woven fabric breathes, or lets water vapour (steam) pass through it. This means people wearing it don't get too hot and sweaty. Even though non-woven fabric breathes, it's also waterproof. No liquids are able to pass through it.

Many workers wear lab coats, overalls or aprons made of non-woven fabric. These work clothes protect workers' regular clothes from things such as oil, grease and paint. People who work with irritating or dangerous materials, such as insulation or poisonous

Overalls made of non-woven fabric, like the suit this man is wearing, can protect people who work with dangerous materials.

chemicals, wear non-woven disposable overalls. They throw them away at the end of the day. Non-woven fabric clothes called scrubs protect medical workers from germs and stop germs from spreading. Doctors and nurses can throw away their scrubs after working with each patient.

Non-woven fabric can be recycled many times. It is used for many other things besides clothes. These things include shipping envelopes, building materials, camping gear and money.

Billboard Bags

Throughout our cities in the United Kingdom you see posters and hoardings, or billboards. All over the world there are hundreds of thousands of these huge signs, usually advertising films, television programmes or computer games.

Film billboards can come in different sizes. The biggest size is the most common. It's 4 metres high and 15 metres wide. That's bigger than the floor space of a two-car garage.

Film billboards are printed on heavy-duty nylon cloth that won't tear. It is coated with vinyl to make it waterproof. The cloth for one billboard can weigh as much as 40 kg. The printed cloth is usually stretched over a frame and fastened in place. Billboard poster ink is made to stay bright for up to eight years in sun, wind and rain. Some billboard posters stay in place for that long. Others stay for just a few months, or even weeks.

Sooner or later, a new film comes out, and the old billboard poster has to come down. Instead of dumping old billboard cloth in landfills, people can recycle it to make useful products.

These bags from Relan, a company in Minnesota, are made from recycled billboard poster fabric.

Billboard companies give or sell their used cloth to manufacturers. The cloth is often dirty and wrinkled. Manufacturers wash and iron the cloth. Workers cut up the cloth to make tote bags, handbags, laptop bags and wallets. The waterproof cloth makes very strong bags. The vinyl coating gives the bags a shiny look.

Billboard bags usually show off bright colours, letters, words or pictures. The letters, words and pictures are so big that only small parts of them show on each bag. People like the bold, colourful look of billboard bags and each bag has a unique design. It is also good to use something that would otherwise end up in a landfill.

Fashionable Rubbish

Companies are making tote bags, handbags and luggage out of many other kinds of rubbish too. One example is used lorry inner tubes, the air-filled rings inside tyres. Inner tubes turn into sleek black handbags, wallets, briefcases, suitcases and belts. The bags and belts look like leather but are washable and waterproof.

Another example is sailcloth from sailing boats. The sails eventually wear out, making them useless for sailing. There's usually plenty of good cloth left to make other things. The strong fabric makes excellent tote bags. At least one company puts a label inside each of its sailcloth bags. The label tells what seas the cloth sailed in its former life.

A company in England makes purses and tote bags from old video and audiotape. Workers knit or crochet the tape using a looped stitch. The workers also make purses from shopping bags the same way. They line the purses and bags with fabric from old clothes or sheets.

Shoes help keep rubbish out of landfills too. New shoes and sandals can be made from old tyres and inner tubes. Because these products are made of rubber, the shoe soles are very strong and long-lasting. The rubber is comfortable to walk on. It also gives the shoes a great grip.

This bag is made out of recycled videotape and audiotape. New products can also be made out of recycled carrier bags.

chapter 2

Making the Most of Muck

Farmers call it manure or dung. Scientists call it excrement or faeces. City workers call it sewage or sludge. Whatever you call it, you have to get rid of it every day. It piles up in places where there are lots of animals or people.

No one wants poo to pile up. It's stinky, ugly and germ-ridden. What can we do with all this muck? People are finding clever new answers to this old question. Even though poo is waste, it still contains nutrients and other valuable things. It can be turned into fertilizer, animal feed, energy and other useful products.

Farm Manure Galore

For thousands of years, farmers have used animal manure to fertilize their fields. The nutrients in manure help plants grow. In the past, most farmers had small numbers of animals. They saved all the manure from

Many farmers use animal waste
to fertilize their crops.

their animals and spread it on their own fields. This helped them make the most of their farms' resources.

Modern farms are different. Many of them keep hundreds or thousands of animals in one place. The animals produce much more manure than their farms can use. The extra manure is a problem because it's not safe to simply throw it away. To solve this problem, farming scientists are thinking up new ways to use manure.

Bedding and Breakfast

Some farms recycle their manure into animal bedding. They must dry and treat the manure to kill germs. This can be expensive, but it saves the cost of buying other bedding. Some scientists worry that too many germs remain in recycled manure bedding. They're studying this idea more to make sure manure bedding is made as safe as possible.

Many cities and towns recycle manure to use in urban spaces and along roadsides. They compost manure (mix it with rotted plants), and road workers spread the compost along roadsides. Compost helps plants grow faster and stronger. The workers then plant grass, shrubs, flowers and other plants along the roadsides.

Another use for manure is animal feed. The manure must, of course, be treated to kill germs and remove other unwanted materials before animals can eat it. Treated manure from cattle, pigs and poultry (farm birds such as chickens and turkeys) is added to all kinds of animal feed. Not all scientists think this is safe. They worry that too many germs could survive the treatment. Other scientists believe it's dangerous to feed animal manure to the same kind of animal it came from.

From Excrement to Electricity

More and more big farms are making electricity from their manure. Electricity made from manure is good for the environment because it's renewable energy. This means the source of the energy can be replaced. As long as there are animals, there will always be plenty of manure! It's also good for the environment because it uses smelly, germ-ridden rubbish that would otherwise just keep piling up.

Most countries make electricity by burning coal or gas. There are two ways to make electricity from manure. One is to burn it directly. The

IT'S A FACT!

Native Americans and pioneers in the central plains of North America in the 1800s burned dried dung for cooking and heat. Herds of bison roaming the plains left behind plenty of the free fuel. Pioneers called the dung 'buffalo chips' or 'meadow muffins'. It was the only fuel they could find on the treeless plains.

Huge turkey farms like this one have to deal with tonnes of manure.

other method is to let the manure rot at first, creating natural gas, and then to burn the gas.

Chicken and turkey manure is best for direct burning. It's pretty dry and contains feathers and bedding as well as faeces. The largest manure-burning electric plant in the world is in England. It burns about 420,000 tonnes of chicken and turkey manure every year. That produces enough electricity for nearly eight thousand homes.

About 800 million broiler chickens are reared in the UK for meat – accounting for 95 per cent of chicken eaten in this country. These birds leave behind over a million tonnes of manure. That manure could make enough electricity to power a whole city.

Cattle and pig manure is much wetter than chicken and turkey manure. Cattle and pig manure would have to be dried before burning, which would be expensive. It's cheaper to turn cattle and pig manure into natural gas. We can burn the gas to heat homes or to make electricity.

Many cattle and pig farms are starting to produce electricity along with milk and meat. To make electricity, the manure goes into a big tank. The tank has a plastic cover. Wet manure enters the tank through a pipe in the

This manure tank is used to turn manure into natural gas.

bottom. New manure, added each day, pushes up the manure already in the tank. By the time manure reaches the top, it has turned into natural gas and liquid. It takes twenty to sixty days to turn manure into natural gas. The gas is piped off for burning, and the liquid is piped off separately for fertilizer.

Some farmers have electric generators on their farms. They make their own electricity from the natural gas they collect. Farmers use the electricity or sell it to their local power companies. Other farmers sell the gas itself to power companies.

There are about ten million cattle and five million pigs in the United Kingdom. They could become important sources of natural gas.

Sewage Solutions

Sewage is different from manure. It includes anything people or factories pour down the drain or flush down the toilet. Sewage contains

Recycling Milk

Another kind of waste from dairy farms is dirty milk. Sometimes mud gets into the milk. Dirty milk can't be sold for people to drink, but farmers can feed this milk to calves.

Unfortunately, the milk often has germs in it that might make calves sick. In the past, farmers usually threw this milk away. However, some farms have started recycling their waste milk by pasteurizing it (heating it to kill germs). Farmers can safely feed pasteurized milk to their calves.

Milk sold for people to drink is also pasteurized. However, farm pasteurization doesn't kill enough germs to make waste milk safe for humans.

everything from faeces and urine to rubbish and dirty water. It also contains dangerous chemicals and harmful metals. It's germy, slimy stuff.

We have to treat sewage to avoid spreading disease and poisoning the environment. Sewage treatment removes dangerous materials. The treatment separates the sewage into liquids and solids. These liquids and solids can be released back into the environment or reused.

Sludge is the name for the solid stuff created by sewage treatment. Every year the United Kingdom gets rid of around 1 million tonnes of sludge. About 15 per cent of it is buried in landfills, 20 per cent is burned and 10 per cent is used in other ways. The rest of it is spread on farmers' fields as fertilizer.

Scientists disagree about whether sludge is safe to spread on fields. Some believe sewage treatment destroys most of the dangerous materials

This worker talks on a walkie-talkie as he keeps on eye on operations at a sewage treatment plant.

contained in it. They also believe that spreading the sludge thinly over large areas of land makes it less risky. Other scientists believe that sludge contains too many dangerous materials. They fear germs and poisons could get in our food through the soil or through water pumped from under the sludge.

Just about everyone agrees, though, that finding a safe use for sludge is better than burying it or burning it.

Zoo Poo

A few paper companies are recycling something very surprising. A company here in the UK is one example. It is helping not only the environment, but also some local zookeepers. This company makes paper out of elephant dung from nearby Woburn Safari Park in Bedfordshire. The park is home to three Asian elephants.

Why make paper out of elephant dung? Asian elephants eat about 100 to 200 kg of food per day. Their bodies have a basic digestive system and they use less than half of the food they eat. The rest is excreted. One elephant can produce over 130 kg of manure every day. That's a lot of manure for a zoo to have to get rid of!

The paper company picks up the manure from the zoo. The zoo workers are glad to donate it. At the paper mill, workers wash, boil and dry the manure. When dry, it looks like dark brown cardboard. Workers then mix it with other recycled paper. The end product is a light-coloured paper that makes fine stationery, notebooks and cards.

This woman mixes elephant dung and paper pulp to make coloured stationery at a recycling plant in Sri Lanka.

Does the elephant dung paper stink?

Apparently not. All the smells and germs in the manure disappear during the washing, boiling and drying process. Most people who buy the paper give it a sniff anyway to make sure.

Pee Power

Scientists in Asia have invented a battery that runs on urine. The battery is a five-layer sandwich about the size of a credit card. In the centre is a chemical-soaked paper. Thin layers of metal sandwich the paper. Two layers of plastic on the outside protect the inner layers.

Each end of the battery has a small slit. A drop of urine placed on the slit soaks into the paper. This starts a chemical reaction that makes electricity. One drop of human urine makes as much electricity as an AA battery for about ten minutes.

Urine-powered batteries can help medical workers in places where there's no electricity. The batteries can run testing machines. The batteries are cheap to make, and there'll never be a shortage of pee to run them!

chapter 3

E-waste and E-cycling

Electronic waste (e-waste) includes unwanted computers, mobile phones and other electronic machines and parts. Recycling e-waste is called e-cycling. E-cycling can mean giving away whole, working electronics for others to use or collecting the valuable parts of electronics for other uses. The useless parts go to landfills.

Every year in the UK about 1 million tonnes of electrical equipment is thrown away by families and businesses. Landfills already contain millions of computers, phones, TVs, video games and other electronics. No one knows how much more of

IT'S A FACT!

E-waste is piling up three times faster than ordinary rubbish. This is partly because electronics go out-of-date so quickly. Manufacturers constantly make better, faster and more powerful machines. Everyone wants the latest model, so older models are hard to resell.

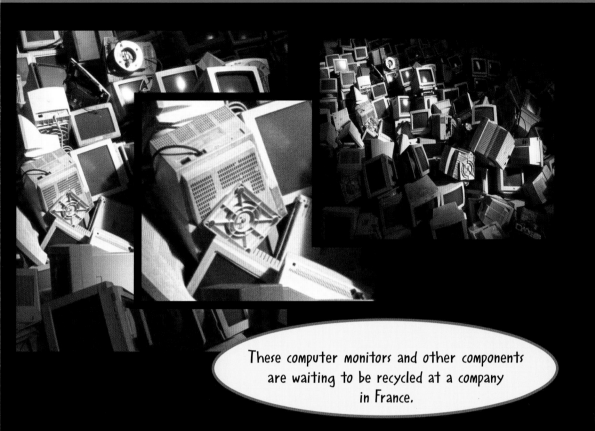

These computer monitors and other components are waiting to be recycled at a company in France.

this stuff is collecting dust on shelves and in closets. Sooner or later, it'll be shoved out of the door with the rest of the rubbish. This all adds up to a mountain-size problem.

E-waste Is Different

E-waste is different from ordinary rubbish because electronics contain metals that can poison us. Lead and mercury are two especially danger-ous metals in e-waste.

Many computer monitors and TV screens contain between 1 and 3.5 kg of lead in their glass. The lead traps harmful radiation (very fast-mov-ing energy) given off by parts inside the monitor or TV. Even though lead can be dangerous, having lead in monitors and TVs is good while they're working.

The Three Rs

You can help cut down on all kinds of waste by following three simple rules:

1. Reduce. Use less. Buy only what you really need. Use up the products you buy. Buy products with less packaging.
2. Reuse. Upgrade your computer rather than buying a new one. Shop with bags from home. Borrow library magazines. Sell or donate useful things you don't want. Buy used things rather than new ones.
3. Recycle. Choose recyclable products. Recycle all the paper, plastic, aluminium foil and glass you can. Compost garden and food waste for fertilizer.

Tell your parents and educate others about the three Rs. Tell shops that you prefer products with less packaging and things that are recycled or recyclable. Volunteer for community recycling efforts.

But when lead glass breaks or burns, lead can escape into the environment. Lead is very poisonous. In the human body, it can cause mental illness, kidney disease and other serious kinds of sickness. When lead glass ends up in landfills, it often breaks, and tiny bits of lead can wash into water supplies and soil. When lead glass burns, the smoke carries lead into people's lungs.

E-waste also contains mercury, another very poisonous metal. Mercury causes some of the same types of health problems as lead, but mercury poisoning is even more serious than lead poisoning. It can cause death much quicker.

E-waste contains more than thirty-five other metals too. These include gold, silver, nickel and copper. Because of all these metals, many landfills no longer accept e-waste. Metals in electronics are hard to get rid of safely. But the metals are valuable if we can get them back. More and more companies are now e-cycling old electronics to collect the precious metals from them.

E-cycling Is Hard Work

One electronic machine may have only tiny amounts of each valuable metal. There's only one way to gather enough metal to sell. That's to take apart hundreds or thousands of machines. Then workers must sort and collect the tiny scraps of metal. This takes a lot of work and time. Some countries, like the United States and Canada for example, ship much of their e-waste to other parts of the world.

An employee sifts through e-waste at a recycling facility in Bangalore, India.

In many underdeveloped or developing countries, workers make much less money than western workers do. It's cheaper for many companies to ship e-waste to these countries than to pay their own native workers to take the machines apart.

Shipping e-waste to other countries has very real problems, though. Many developing countries do not have laws to protect their workers or the environment. Their workers may not know about the dangers of lead, mercury or other harmful metals. They may let these poisons into the air, soil, water or even their bodies without knowing it.

Some rich nations are dumping dangerous e-waste in Africa. It is thought that most of the world's 50 million tonnes of e-waste ends up in Africa, India or China, disposed of by unethical recycling firms or

This sign at an office supply shop tells customers that it can recycle their old electronics.

Recycle your old phone, pager or handheld here.

'e-waste cowboys' as charitable donations. Some electronics makers now have e-waste return services. People who buy new electronics from these companies can send their old electronics to the company for e-cycling.

Even after e-cycling the valuable parts from e-waste, there's still a lot left over. Many electronic parts are made of flame-retardant plastic. Special chemicals in the plastic make it difficult to burn. These chemicals also make the plastic hard to recycle. These parts usually end up in landfills.

E-waste is also known as WEEE in the United Kingdom, standing for Waste Electrical and Electronic Equipment. Two key pieces of legislation affecting e-waste or WEEE are in the process of being introduced in the United Kingdom. Local authorities are setting up collection or take-back schemes which allow users to return their waste electronic products free of charge. The United Kingdom is also setting itself recycling targets of collecting 4kg of electronic waste per person per year. According to new laws, companies producing and importing electronic and electrical products are going to be legally and financially responsible for their disposal.

chapter 4

New Uses for Old Tyres

Every year people in the UK throw away around 475,000 tonnes of tyres. Around 20 per cent of these tyres are repaired and put back on cars, 34 per cent are recycled. Tyres cannot be put into household waste or burned.

Stockpiling tyres is bad for the environment because tyres attract pests. In some countries mosquitoes breed in rainwater trapped in tyres. Mice and rats nest in tyres. These pests spread dangerous diseases.

Millions of old tyres are stockpiled and burned in many plants in the USA to make electricity.

Stockpiled tyres can also cause enormous problems if they catch fire. Burning tyres give off dangerous gases, metals and oil. An average car tyre when burned gives off more than 7 litres of oil. One million tyres burning produce about 210,000 litres of oil. If the oil gets into water sources, it poisons the water and harms the environment.

Spanish firefighters help one another while trying to put out a fire at an illegal tyre dump in 2003.

Tyre Fires

Tyres are hard to set on fire, but once they start burning, tyre fires are hard to put out. Water and firefighting foam don't help much. Bulldozers must push sand or soil onto the burning tyres to smother the flames.

In 1983 a stockpile of seven million tyres in Virginia, USA caught fire. The smoke spread out for 80 kms (50 miles) and travelled to three different states. It rose around 900 metres into the air. The fire burned for nine months.

People start most tyre fires, either on purpose or by accident. Lightning can start a tyre fire, but it only happens very rarely.

About 12 per cent of UK scrap tyres end up in landfills. That's about 57, 000 tonnes of tyres every year. Tyres cause problems in landfills. They take up lots of space. They also trap air underground because of their shape. Over time the tyres can work their way to the surface, pulling up rotten waste with them.

UK laws say that tyres must be shredded before going into landfills, although proposals were made in 2007 to ban putting tyres in landfills in any form. Currently in some places, tyres go into monofills (landfills that allow only one type of rubbish). It's better to put tyres in a monofill than to put them in an ordinary landfill or to stockpile them in the open. In a monofill, they're buried so they can't burn or attract pests.

Finding new uses for scrap tyres is better than putting them into monofills. There are many uses for old tyres. Most of these uses require chopping the tyres into shredded (crumb) rubber. Recycling companies chop the tyres down to different sizes for different uses.

This man holds shredded rubber from car tyres. Manufacturers can use this rubber to make many products.

Rubber Roads

The biggest use of scrap tyres is in road building. Road workers can use chopped tyres in different ways. The most common use is for asphalt rubber, which uses up millions of tyres every year. Asphalt rubber combines shredded or crumb rubber with asphalt (a tarry black material). Workers heat them together to make road surfaces. A two-lane road with an asphalt rubber surface 5 cm thick uses up four thousand tyres per 1.6 km (per 1 mile).

Asphalt rubber surfaces last longer than normal asphalt. Asphalt begins to get brittle and cracks over time. Water runs into the cracks and seeps under the road. This excess water causes potholes and breaks up the road. Adding rubber helps the road surface bend and stretch instead of crack. Asphalt rubber roads don't need to be fixed as often as normal asphalt roads.

Another important road-building use of scrap tyres is for roads in cold places. During the spring, melting snow and rain soak the ground, and extra water collects under roads. This water freezes and melts several times, breaking up the road. With a layer of shredded tyres under the surface, the water will not freeze. This saves a lot of time, work and money on fixing the roads.

IT'S A FACT!

Roads made with rubber are quiet. People first noticed this in Belgium in 1981. Since then, tests have shown that cars make half as much noise on asphalt rubber roads as they do on other roads.

IT'S A FACT!

Rubber gives roads really good grip. Drivers can stop their cars in less time on asphalt rubber roads than on other types of roads.

People can use shredded rubber for other surfaces besides roads. For example, floors made of recycled rubber can look like tile or stone. Rubber floors are comfortable to walk on and prevent slipping. They last for many years and can be recycled again. Shredded rubber can be combined with other materials to make sports tracks and fields. Rubber fields and tracks are easier to care for than grass.

Rubber mulch is another product made from shredded rubber. It makes a good playground surface because it's springy. When used in gardens, it holds moisture in the soil. Another use for rubber mulch is in horse arenas. Horse handlers like it because it's easy on horses' feet and legs.

However, recycled rubber has some drawbacks. Rubber can get very hot in the sun – hot enough to melt shoe soles! Some rubber sports fields and tracks use sprinkling systems to keep them cool. If rubber mulch catches fire, the flames are hard to put out. Rubber mulch can also contain poisonous metals and chemicals. These can get into soil or water.

This family plays on the swings in their garden. They used recycled rubber for the play area's surface.

Tyres for Energy

Around 15 per cent of scrap tyres in the UK are burned as fuel for businesses. Tyres are not so good for heating homes. They must be burned in closed furnaces so their smoke and oil don't escape into the environment.

Tyres can be burned either shredded or whole. Tyres provide about the same amount of energy as oil. They provide more energy than coal and also burn cleaner than most coal.

Electric companies burn about thirty-four million tyres every year. Businesses burn another seventeen million tyres a year to heat their buildings. The tyres heat water that's piped through the buildings. Some factories, such as cement and paper factories, burn tyres for energy to run their machines.

This California power plant was the first US plant to use whole tyres for making electricity.

More Tyre Inventions

More and more companies are finding new ways to use old tyres. Tyre bits can replace soil for many uses. They can fill in wet areas so workers can build roads through swamps. They can build up the sides of walls, roads and bridges. They can replace stone to help rainwater drain away from buildings. They even cover up rubbish in landfills that do not accept whole tyres.

This road on Mayotte Island in the Indian Ocean runs alongside a barrier made of tyres.

People are finding new ways to recycle whole tyres too. Car racetracks use them as crash barriers. Farmers use extra-large tyres to hold hay bales in place under silage sheets. Families use them for planters, sandpits and swings.

The Osborne Reef Disaster

Artificial reefs (undersea structures) provide homes for fish and other sea animals, such as barnacles, corals, sponges and oysters. Sunken vehicles and pieces of buildings make good artificial reefs. In 1974 a company used old tyres to enlarge Osborne Reef off the coast of Fort Lauderdale, Florida, USA. The US Navy and many private boats helped. A tyre company lent tools for the project.

Workers dropped two million tyres strapped with steel clips into the sea. No animals ever moved in. The clips broke, and the tyres separated. They started to drift, crashing into and damaging natural coral and rock reefs. Hurricanes tossed thousands of tyres onto Florida beaches. No one knew how far some had travelled.

In 2007 a cleanup of this failed project began.

Turning Rubbish Into Crude Oil

Rubbish has less value than anything on Earth. In fact, rubbish is so worthless, it's actually expensive to keep it around. It costs billions of pounds a year to take care of something that nobody wants! To solve this problem, scientists are working on ways to turn rubbish into oil, one of the most valuable materials on our planet.

Crude oil is a dark liquid found far underground. People refine it to make petrol, fuel oil, plastic, fabric, fertilizer and thousands of other products. Crude oil is so valuable, it's sometimes called black gold.

Some crude oil is found under the ocean floor. This oil rig pumps oil and sends it through an undersea pipeline to oil refineries.

The main chemical building blocks of crude oil are carbon and hydrogen. These are the main building blocks of all living things. Over thousands of years, the Earth's heat and pressure on dead plants and animals buried underground formed crude oil. As the Earth takes such a long time to make oil naturally, crude oil is not a renewable energy source.

Rubbish is made of the same things as crude oil. It's mostly dead plants and animals in the form of paper, leaves, food, plastic, rubber, leather, cloth and wood. What if we could put heat and pressure on rubbish to make crude oil? What if we could do it in hours rather than thousands of years? If we could do it fast enough, we could turn piles of our most worthless junk into barrels of our most valuable liquid.

Several universities and businesses are trying out different ways of making crude oil from rubbish. One idea is turning pig manure to oil in a way that removes all the smell. Another idea is turning manure and vegetable waste into oil. Some cities have proposed turning sewage sludge into oil. If these ideas work, crude oil will become a renewable energy source.

Oil from Animals

One business in Missouri, USA is already making oil from rubbish. It is next door to one of the biggest turkey processing plants in the country. The plant processes thirty thousand turkeys every day. This creates around 180 tonnes of waste a day. The waste includes skin, bones, fat, intestines, organs, feet, heads, feathers and blood.

This gruesome waste goes into a huge grinder first. The grinder finely chops everything up and adds water. The waste comes out a greyish

Construction on this waste-to-fuel plant (*top*) began in late 2006. Plants like this are working hard to turn waste into clean fuel (*bottom*).

brown liquid. This liquid flows through a series of tanks that heat it, put pressure on it, then cool it. This breaks down the turkey parts and changes them into oil. The heating time is about fifteen minutes at about 260°C. The whole process from raw waste to crude oil takes about two hours.

From about 1 tonne of turkey waste, the plant can make 270 kg of high-grade crude oil similar to diesel fuel. The plant can make an impressive 80,000 litres of oil a day. The oil can be refined more to make petroleum or kerosene. The oil-making process also creates useful things such as natural gas and fertilizer. The used water is recycled back into the plant.

The Missouri waste-to-fuel plant opened in 2004. The next year, Missouri's governor ordered the plant to close because people complained about its smell. The plant quickly took steps to control the smell and started up again. Plant officials say it costs about as much to make oil in their plant as it does to explore and drill for natural crude oil, without harming the environment.

This waste-to-fuel process kills all the germs in the waste. It also removes or grinds up metals, sharp objects and other difficult items fairly easily. That means this process could be used to make oil from household waste, medical waste, hazardous waste, e-waste, tyres and sewage sludge without danger to people.

If just the farm waste produced in the United States could be turned into oil, it would create four billion barrels of oil per year. That's about how much oil they buy from other countries every year. They'd need to build waste-to-oil plants all over the country, which would take a lot of work and money. Many scientists and government leaders believe the change would be worth the effort.

Oil from Plastic

Plants in the United Kingdom and Japan have been turning used plastic into fuel since the 1990s. Like the waste-to-oil process, this process also uses grinding, heat and pressure. Unlike other kinds of plastic recycling, the plastic-to-oil process doesn't require sorting or washing. It can use all sorts of plastic – even plastics that are not usually recycled.

A plastic-to-oil plant can process up to 20 tonnes of plastic per day. This produces about 20,000 litres of oil. This high-grade oil works in any engine that can burn artificial fuel. Some of the plastic-to-oil plants

Hazardous Waste

Some kinds of rubbish are too dangerous to put into ordinary landfills. This type of rubbish is called hazardous waste. Household hazardous waste includes paint, cleaning liquids, motor oil, batteries and pesticides. Industrial hazardous waste includes many chemicals used in factories and mining. Hazardous waste must go to special landfills that keep the dangerous materials away from the environment.

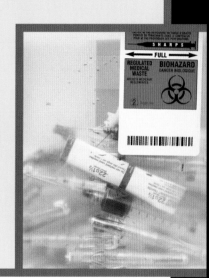

Medical waste is a special kind of hazardous waste. It includes things that have blood on them, such as needles and other medical tools. It also includes parts of people's bodies removed in surgery. Blood and flesh contain germs that could spread diseases. Medical waste must be burned or sterilized (to kill germs) before going to a landfill.

Medical waste, such as these used syringes, is a kind of hazardous waste.

have electric generators built into them, so they can produce electrical power as well as oil.

The Nature of Recycling

Oil buried under the Earth is a result of natural recycling. Thousands of years ago, the earth recycled dead plants and animals to form oil. Recycling is an important part of nature.

Humans are doing the same thing. People are turning unwanted materials into oil and other useful things. We're learning the importance of the three Rs – reducing, reusing and recycling. When we recycle, we help nature and when we help nature, we help ourselves.

aluminium: a lightweight, silvery metal often used for drink cans

bale: a big, tightly-bound bundle

compost: a mixture of rotted leaves, vegetables or manure used to enrich soil and help plants grow

crude oil: a thick, oily liquid found underground, used to make petrol, fuel oil, plastic and many other products

dung: solid waste from animals

excrement: solid waste from animals and people

faeces: solid waste from animals and people

flame-retardant: hard to burn

generator: a machine that produces electricity

hazardous waste: dangerous rubbish that needs special handling to be safely thrown away

industrial waste: rubbish from factories and mining

infrared sensor: a tool that detects differences in light that human eyes cannot see

landfill: a place where waste is buried or contained so that it will not harm the surrounding environment

medical waste: rubbish from medical clinics and hospitals, much of which contains blood and other germ-ridden material

monofill: a landfill that accepts only one kind of rubbish

nutrient: any material that people, animals or plants need to stay strong and healthy

pasteurize: to heat a liquid to a temperature high enough to kill germs

polyester: a kind of cloth made from artificial plastic thread

polyethylene terephthalate (PET-1 or PETE): a kind of plastic used mostly to make cloth, insulation and clear plastic bottles and containers for drinks and food

radiation: tiny parts that break off from materials, causing harmful, very fast-moving rays of energy. Radiation cannot be seen, heard or felt, but can cause very serious illness.

recycle: to process used or unwanted items so they can be made into new products

recycling centre: a plant that processes waste for reuse

renewable energy: energy from sources that cannot be used up, such as wind, waves or sunlight, or that can be replaced, such as plants and manure

rubber mulch: a ground cover made from chopped or shredded tyres

sewage: liquid and solid waste carried away in drains and toilets

sewage sludge: solid matter left over after sewage treatment

spinneret: a machine with many holes in it, through which liquid is forced to form strands that harden and can be twisted into thread

sterilized: cleaned so thoroughly that all germs are killed

urine: liquid waste from animals and people

WEEE: stands for Waste Electrical and Electronic Equipment

X-ray: an invisible kind of energy that can pass through solid objects

American Plastics Council. 'Plastic Packaging Resins'. *American Chemistry Council Plastics Division Learning Center.* 2007. http://www.americanchemistry.com/s_plastics/bin.asp?CID=1102&DID=4645&DOC= FILE.PDF (27 February 2007).

Dubanowitz, Alexander. 'Design of a Materials Recovery Facility (MRF) for Processing the Recyclable Materials of New York City's Municipal Solid Waste'. *Columbia University Earth Engineering Center.* May 2000. http://www.seas.columbia.edu/earth/dubanmrf.pdf (28 November 2006).

Halweil, Brian. 'Plastic Bags'. *Worldwatch Institute Publications: Good Stuff?* 2006. http://www.worldwatch.org/node/1499 (27 November 2006).

Lee, Ki Bang. 'Urine-Activated Paper Batteries for Biosystems'. *Journal of Micromechanics and Microengineering.* August 15, 2005. http://www.iop.org/EJ/abstract/0960-1317/15/9/S06 (7 December 2006).

Lemley, Brad. 'Anything into Oil'. *Discover.* May 2003, 50–57.

National Association for PET Container Resources. *NAPCOR Website.* 2004. http://www.napcor.com (29 November 2006).

National Recovery Technologies. 'High-Speed Identification and Sorting of Plastic Resin Flake for Recycling'. *Small Business Innovation Research Success Stories.* 27 November, 2006. http://es.epa.gov/ncer/sbir/success/pdf/highspeed.pdf (5 December 2006).

Royte, Elizabeth. 'E-gad!' *Smithsonian.* August 2005, 82–86.

Royte, Elizabeth. *Garbage Land: On the Secret Trail of Trash.* New York: Little, Brown and Company, 2005.

Tufts University. 'History and Statistics of US Waste Production and Recycling'. *Tufts Recycles! Facts Pages.* N.d. http://www.tufts.edu/tuftsrecycles/USstats.htm (27 November 2006).